S T U D E N T

Y0-CCT-109

VITAL
BELIEFS

FINDING OUR PLACE IN
THE STORY OF GOD

JIM HAMPTON and
MIKE SCHOONOVER

EDITORS
D'Wayne Leatherland and Jeff Edmondson

ASSISTANT EDITOR
Edie MacPherson

COVER DESIGN
Kevin Williamson

INSIDE ILLUSTRATIONS
D'lan Davidson

Copyright 2001
by WordAction Publishing Company

ISBN 083-411-7363

Printed in the
United States of America

CONTENTS

BEFORE YOU START

We are so glad you have picked up this book. It's our hope that you will have a close encounter with God as you read and study this book. We believe the Lord wants to meet with you in a special way as you read. If you listen for His voice, He will speak to His children. The Bible says that Jesus' kids (sheep) know His voice, and they will follow Him (John 10:4).

A woman and a man were walking through the busy streets of New York City. With horns blowing and hundreds of feet pounding the pavement, the man stopped and said, "Did you hear that?"

"What?" his friend questioned.

"I hear a cricket."

"How in the world can you hear a cricket? You're crazy!"

The man walked over to some flowers in front of a window, pulled them back, and there was a cricket.

"I don't understand," said the woman. "How could you hear a single, tiny cricket?"

"Well," he said, "you usually hear what you are listening for. Watch this." Reaching into his pocket, he pulled out a coin and tossed it on the sidewalk. Everybody within a few feet stopped and looked down at the ringing coin.

You see, in a world full of noise and confusion, you will only hear what you are listening for. If you are like most teenagers, you lead an extremely busy life. School, church, extracurricular activities, and a job all take up your time. However, if you want to hear God's voice, if you really seek Him, He will speak to you in really cool ways. Take a moment right now to stop and affirm to yourself and to God that you really want to hear from Him as you read this book. You'll be glad you did.

Why Is This Book Important?

This book deals with the crucial issues of our Christian faith. Why is this important? Simply put, if you don't know what you stand for and why, you will be susceptible to every false teaching

5

that comes along. While working through this book you'll have the opportunity to come to grips with what you believe and why you believe it through reading real-life scenarios, searching the Scriptures, and making personal application. In short, this book has three specific purposes: (1) to affirm your faith; (2) to help you understand your faith; and (3) to help you defend your faith.

HOW TO USE THIS BOOK

We have decided to use icons (pictures that act as symbols) to mark the various sections of each chapter. Following is each icon and its description.

 To Quote gives two quotes on the topic. One quote is by John Wesley (our theological forefather) and the other is by a contemporary scholar. These are designed to stimulate your thinking.

 Real Life is a true-to-life scenario that helps put the topic in context. It will serve as an introduction to the topic being discussed.

 Your Life gives you an opportunity to examine where you are in relation to the topic at hand. It's always important to examine our own beliefs first, so that we know where we need to grow.

 Theology 101 is the heart of the chapter. There, the topic will be discussed more in depth and in language that makes sense.

 Look It Up is a short scripture study to help you see what the Bible says. While it will be tempting to skip this section, we urge you to complete it. Reading and studying God's Word is crucial to understanding the basics of the Christian faith.

 Why Should I Care? is the application section. It attempts to answer the question, "Why is this topic important to me?"

 My Place in the Story helps you understand how each chapter's topic assists you in finding your place in the Story of God.

Did You Know? is a sidebar that lists both important and fun facts about the topic.

 Big Words lists some of the big theological words that Christians have traditionally used to talk about their faith. We've done our best to write these definitions with words you can understand.

 Giving It to God is a short prayer you can offer to God to help you apply the topic. It is written in simple, honest language, and hopefully, will come from your heart.

 Take It with You presents a scripture verse (or two) for you to memorize. God's Word promises that when we commit His Word to our hearts, it will be like a lamp that lights our way.

 Dig Deeper gives reading suggestions if you want to study the topic further. We hope you will.

Suggestions for Studying This Book

As you read this book, we invite you to read it a little differently than you would most books. Following are some ideas to help you better understand what you read.

1. Find a quiet, secluded place away from all distractions. Reading this while watching TV will probably not be the most productive. Remember, real reading is like sports—you get out of it what you put into it. Give it your all for this short book, and see what happens.
2. Take a deep breath once you find your study place. Slow down, maybe close your eyes, and begin by talking to God in your own words. Whatever you pray is cool, but be sure to invite God to hang out with you.
3. Read slowly! This isn't for a book report about something you don't care about. You really do care about this one, so take it easy. Engage that brain of yours. Open your heart. Say out loud that you want to be teachable during your study time.

8

4. When you read something that rocks your world, stop. Think about it, and let it soak in. Read it again—maybe even read it out loud. We learn best through repetition, and nothing is worth repeating more than God's Word.
5. Remember that the goal is formation, not information. Many people know the Word, but as Christians, our goal is to not only know the Word but also live the Word. Formation simply means allowing the text to shape your life. The Scriptures are meant to reveal to us spiritual realities we should "live" out.
6. Be obedient. Let's be honest—obedience isn't always easy. But if we want God to work in our lives, we have to be obedient. Commit yourself to obey whatever God shows you. You might even want to tell a close friend, and ask him or her to keep you accountable.
7. Spend time in prayer. Ask God to help you concentrate as you read. Pray for wisdom to understand what you read. And finally, commit to God that you will respond to what He tells you.

FINDING OUR PLACE IN THE STORY OF GOD

God's Story

Whether or not we realize it, each of us lives according to a story. And the story we live by has a significant impact on how we act, think, and speak.

The people of Israel were used to hearing false stories. They had lived in bondage in Egypt for decades. Pharaoh and his army had repeatedly told the Israelites they were no more than slaves, people of little worth. Though it was a lie, the Israelites had heard it for so long that they began to act accordingly.

In a similar way, you and I are living in a cultural "Egypt." There are a number of false stories the world (Pharaoh) offers us as though they were true: look out for number one; live only for the moment; he who dies with the most toys wins; if you're going to make it, it's up to you; it doesn't really matter what you believe since all religions are the same. Far too often, we end up adopting these stories as our own.

The people of Israel would have continued living under their false stories if God had not sent Moses. Moses reminded them that they were the people of God and, as a result, they were called to live according to a different Story.

When we ask Jesus Christ into our hearts we are not only forgiven of our sins but also invited to abandon the false stories that the world offers and to live according to God's Story. This is the Story that begins with the creation of Adam and Eve; includes the call of Moses and Abraham; the kingship of David; the rise of the prophets; the life, death, and resurrection of Christ; and continues with the rise of the Church. But the Story of God doesn't end there. It continues to this day as new members are brought into the family of God. This Story includes you and me.

Living in the Story of God is a radical way of life. It's much *more* than just making God our first priority, thinking that as long as we keep Christ first in our lives then everything else will fall into place. The problem with this line of thinking is this: When we place God at the top of our priority list, the list is still *ours*.

God wants to take over our list and make it His. Furthermore, He wants us to make our lives His. Rather than inviting God into our story, God invites us into His Story.

Let me illustrate it this way. The church I attend does a reenactment of the life of Christ every Easter. Over 100 people are involved, each one wearing period costumes. Live animals are brought in and authentic sets are built, replicating the town of Jerusalem.

When the drama starts, the actors come in from the back of the sanctuary. As they move toward the stage, the actors pass through the audience, interacting with them. They try to sell pots, bread, and fruit to the audience members. In addition, the actors stop and chat with members of the audience, talking about the events happening in Jerusalem. By the time the actors reach the stage, the audience isn't merely observing a story. They are *in* the story.

Similarly, when we become Christians, it's not enough for us to just be passive bystanders, waiting for Christ to work in our lives. Instead, we are called to be active participants with God, placing our lives in His Story and allowing His will to become ours. It's in this Story that we ultimately find our identity as children of God.

Finding our place in the Story of God is of prime importance. However, it's also important that we recognize our theological roots, since these roots have a direct impact on how we will understand the vital beliefs that are the subject of this book.

The Wesleyan-Holiness Story

A couple of centuries ago there lived a young man named John Wesley. I imagine he was a lot like us. He'd been raised in church, had heard hundreds of sermons, and had even participated in a mission trip or two. Yet he still lacked a real, vital, living faith. Even though his dad was a preacher, he still had not understood what it meant to have faith.

While participating in a mission trip to the Native Americans in North America, Wesley realized this. In his journal he wrote, "I went to America, to convert the Indians; but O! who shall convert me?"[1] He had come face-to-face with his own lack of faith.

Later, back home in London on May 24, 1738, Wesley went to a Bible study. There, he heard someone read Martin Luther's preface to the Book of Romans. Wesley described in his journal what happened: "About a quarter before nine, while he was describing the change which God works in the heart through faith in Christ, I felt my heart strangely warmed. I felt I did trust in Christ, Christ alone for my salvation: And an assurance was given me that he had taken away *my* sins, even *mine,* and saved *me* from the law of sin and death."[2]

In that moment Wesley developed a real, vital, and living faith that was his own. He became serious about his faith. No longer was he content to just trust what everyone else said about God. Instead, he diligently studied God's Word and spent time in prayer in an effort to know God better. Because of Wesley's faith, many others came to know God as their personal Savior.

Wesley's contributions to the Christian faith became the foundation for much of what Wesleyan-Holiness churches believe today. This book is written for those who fall under that faith story.

My Story

As the Story of God and the story of our faith tradition continues to be written, you and I have the opportunity to contribute to those stories. But before we can do this, we must know both stories well enough that our own stories are shaped by them. It is my prayer that as you read this book these vital beliefs will shape *your* faith story in order that it may become an integral part of the Story of God.

1

The Trinity
This Is *Not* a Rock Band!

 **Real Life**

Lisa was frustrated. As they had sat together in the cafeteria at school, she had been trying to explain what it meant to be a Christian to her best friend, Chamique. Unfortunately, Chamique was having a hard time understanding who God is.

"Now, tell me again," Chamique said. "You say that you only believe in one God. Yet you also say that you believe that Jesus is God and the Holy Spirit is God? Isn't that a contradiction?"

Lisa replied, "I know it may seem like we are worshiping three Gods, but we don't. There is only one God. But He chooses to reveal himself to us in different ways."

"But how can you say you only believe in one God and yet also claim that God is three people named Father, Jesus, and the Holy Spirit?"

"I know it seems confusing," Lisa said, "but you just have to have faith."

"I don't know. It seems awfully hard to say I have faith in something that doesn't seem to be logical at all," Chamique stated.

Lisa was clearly exasperated by this turn in the conversation.

But, she admitted to herself, even though it was difficult explaining the concept of God being three in one, she still hadn't quite figured out what difference it really made for her own life. *Oh well*, she thought, *maybe somebody else can help Chamique understand this.*

Have you ever felt like Lisa? Trying to explain to others (whether or not they are Christians) the concept of God being three separate people yet also being just one (commonly referred to as the "Trinity") seems impossible. In fact, a prominent scholar once put it this way: "It has been said that while one may be in danger of losing his soul by denying the doctrine of the Trinity, he is in equal danger of losing his wits if he tries to understand it."[1]

Let us put your mind at ease right now—we're not going to cause you to lose your wits! Simply put, no one can *fully* explain the concept of the Trinity. Yet, it's important for Christians to understand what we can, because this belief in the Trinity is central to our faith. Let's examine what the Bible and theology can tell us about this three-in-one God.

🆈🆃 Your Life

1. In 50 words or less, describe who God is.

   He is the supremoe of all Gods. He also takes care of us as watching all of us.

2. Why do you think it's so important to understand the concept of the Trinity?

   So if you get the concept but yet not to understand it you know its only one person.

3. Based on your current understanding, how would you explain the concept of the Trinity to a friend?

   That God is a three-in-one God.

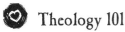 **Theology 101**

The Bible affirms both that God is one and that God is three. It doesn't try to prove that God is both three and one; it simply takes it for granted.

The word "Trinity" does not mean three gods who exist together to make up God (referred to as tritheism). Instead, Trinity refers to the fact that while there is only one God, that God has three eternal and coequal persons. All share the same essence and substance, but each one has a distinct existence. According to the Bible, those three persons are God the Father, God the Son (Jesus Christ), and God the Spirit (Holy Spirit).

Belief in one God is called monotheism. Atheism is the belief that there is no God. And polytheism is the belief in more than one God. Christians are monotheists, because we do not worship three Gods, but one God in three persons.

Confused? Let's look at a couple of illustrations to see if they can help us better understand this concept.

Think about water for a moment. Water can exist in three forms: a solid (ice), a liquid (water), and a gas (steam). Each form looks and acts distinctly different. Yet, regardless of the form it takes, all three are still the same H_2O molecule.

Let's try one more. Every government has three tasks or functions: making laws, administering the laws, and punishing those who break the laws. In the United States, these three functions are performed by the Congress, the president and his cabinet, and the court system. Although these are three distinct groups, all of them are a part of the one government.

In the same way, the Father, the Son, and the Holy Spirit are each unique, but God is also one entity.

Still confused? That's OK. The Trinity is truly one of the great mysteries of Christianity. And while we may not fully understand it, we can affirm the concept because Scripture affirms it.

Look It Up

1. Look up each of the following scriptures and write down what you think they tell us about the concept of the Trinity: Genesis 1:26; Deuteronomy 6:4; Matthew 3:16-17; 28:19-20; John 1:1-18; 14:15-17.

2. Let's examine the roles of each member of the Trinity and see how they are similar.

   a. God, the Father: Genesis 1:1; John 3:16-19

   b. God, the Son: Colossians 1:16; Mark 10:45

   c. God, the Holy Spirit: Psalm 104:30; Titus 3:3-6

 ## Big Words

Arianism—A belief in one God, but not believing that Jesus or the Holy Spirit are divine.

Monotheism—The belief in one true God.

Sabellianism—An anti-Trinitarian belief that teaches that the Father, Son, and Spirit do not exist at the same time, but that each one existed at a certain period in history (i.e., God in the Old Testament, Jesus in the New Testament, and the Spirit in the present).

Trinity—A theological term to express the biblical teaching that God is one and yet three: Father, Son, and Holy Spirit.

Did You Know?
The word "Trinity" never appears in Scripture. This term was created in A.D. 325 by a group of church leaders at the Council of Nicea. These church members were concerned about those who misrepresented the proper relationship between God, Jesus, and the Holy Spirit.

 ## Why Should I Care?

What difference does it make whether or not you believe in the Trinity? A lot. Each member of the Trinity has one purpose in mind—to free us from our sin and restore our relationship with God (which we will discuss further in chapters 3 and 4). This triune God has been working since the beginning of time to make a way for all of us to have an intimate relationship with Him. And when this happens, we can finally become the people that God always intended for us to be.

My Place in the Story

When we are called into the Story of God, we are called into one, singular story. We don't live according to multiple stories, but our lives are shaped and formed by the Story of God. God is calling you today to assume your rightful place in this Story.

 ### Take It with You

May the grace of the Lord Jesus Christ, and the love of God, and the fellowship of the Holy Spirit be with you all (2 Corinthians 13:14).

 ## Giving It to God

Pray this prayer: *God, I have to tell You that this Trinity thing is awfully confusing. I'm not sure that I really understand it. But I do trust Your Word, and so I ask You to help me believe in the Trinity. Through Your Holy Spirit, give me the wisdom and faith to hold to this important truth. In Jesus' name. Amen.*

Dig Deeper

Here are some books that will be helpful if you want to do more studying on this important topic:

- *The Trinity: Is the Doctrine Biblical—Is It Important?* by F. Donald Harris (Neptune, N.J.: Loizeaux Brothers, 2001). (087-213-3109)

    This is a concise look at the doctrine of the Trinity. An excellent introduction for new believers.

- *Three in One: A Picture of God* by Joanne Marxhausen (St. Louis: Concordia Publishing House, 1984). (057-007-7907)

    Written for children, this clever book helps you understand the concept of the Trinity through the use of everyday objects.

2

The Bible

Much More than Your Average Best-Seller!

 **Real Life**

Tom, the youth leader at Christ Church, had just finished teaching the youth group on the importance of reading the Bible. When he finished, he asked, "How many of you read your Bible on a daily basis?"

As Tom looked around, he noticed that no one had raised a hand. And so Tom, thinking that they must not have understood him, asked again, "Come on. The question is simple: How many of you read your Bible every day?" This time there were a few nervous coughs as students looked around, but again no one raised a hand.

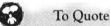 **To Quote**

Most people who don't believe the Bible have never read it!
—Paul E. Little, 20th-century professor and apologist

The Spirit of God not only once inspired those who wrote it, but continually inspires, supernaturally assists, those that read it with earnest prayer.
—John Wesley, 18th-century English evangelist and the father of Wesleyan theology

Tom decided to take a different approach. He asked, "All right, if none of you read your Bible every day, how often do you read it?" A few students volunteered that they read their Bible a couple of times a week.

Tom was amazed. He didn't understand why no one was taking Bible reading seriously. And so he said, "Why don't you all read your Bibles?"

After a few minutes of awkward silence, one of the students,

Evan, spoke up. "To be honest, I find it boring. Who really cares about who begat who?"

"For me," said Marvin, "it's that I'm really busy and don't have time to read it."

"Yeah," echoed Patty, "I can always think of something I would rather be doing."

Finally Rhonda spoke up. "Besides, who wants to read something that doesn't seem to make sense? When I read the Bible, it seems like it is written in a different language."

Tom just sighed. He knew that he had a huge job in front of him.

Do you relate to the sentiments expressed by any of the teens? Have you ever struggled with reading the Bible, because it seems boring? Or maybe you were interested but just didn't think you had time to read it? Maybe you like reading the Bible but you just have a tough time understanding it. If any of these fits you, then this chapter is for you.

🌐 Your Life

1. Circle which of the following words best describes how you feel about reading the Bible: excited, frustrated, bored, anxious, a waste of time, rewarding.

2. What do you think the purpose of reading the Bible is?

3. In your opinion, what makes the Bible such an important book?

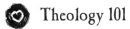 Theology 101

Is it possible that something written over 3,000 years ago could really make a difference in our lives? Not just a "Wow, that was a fun book with good stories" difference but a "Wow, that Book was written about me and for me" life-changing difference! Consider the Bible as a personal love letter from the One who knows us better than we know ourselves, and yet still chooses to love us. This Book tells us that this same God can free us from all of our sins. In addition, it gives us the details about how we can become the complete (missing nothing) people that God created us to be! I think many of us who have always had two or three Bibles somewhere around the house have forgotten how out of this world and powerful this Book really is!

The Bible is a book unlike any other book, because it is from God himself. No, it didn't fall out of the sky or just suddenly appear. Over a long period of time, God actually gave specific thoughts to many different men to write down. God helped guide these men on how to best communicate His message of love and salvation. There-fore, it's appropriate to say that God is the real Author. This is what is meant when the Bible is called the "inspired" Word of God.

God designed His Word for everyone. The Bible is meant for you just as much as it was meant for your great-great-grandparents way back when. It will also have meaning for your children someday. The Bible will never be outdated like your old clothes or CDs, but it will continue to be relevant regardless of the time.

Reading God's Word is not enough. That's only half of the equation. The other half (and just as important) is obeying what we read. It does us no good whatsoever if we read the Bible and never act on it. But when we allow what we read to shape and transform us as we seek to obey, then God's Word truly becomes living and active.

In order to understand the Bible, we need to know how to read it. Follow these tips to help you read and understand God's Word.

- Choose a Bible translation that you can understand.
- Start with a book of the Bible that is easier to understand (I suggest Mark or James).
- Begin with prayer.
- Before you begin to read the particular passage, look for the big picture of the biblical book. Discover who the author was, who he was writing to, and why.

- Read one section at a time. Our modern Bibles have been broken into sections and given headings that help us know what each section is about. Each section contains a complete story or thought.
- Read through the passage several times in order to get the overall picture.
- Decide what the main point is.
- Write down any questions you have regarding this passage. Look to see if the passage offers any answers to your questions. If the passage itself doesn't give answers, consult various commentaries or even your pastor(s) and teacher(s).
- Apply the truth. Put it into practice. Let God's Word change your life.

Look It Up

Take a moment to look up 2 Timothy 3:16-17 and answer these questions.

1. Why is Scripture something that we should obey?

2. What is Scripture useful for (its benefits)?

Why Should I Care?

Why is it important that we regularly read the Bible? Simply put, it's like a relationship with your best friend. The more time you spend getting to know each other, the closer the relationship. The same is true of God. The more we know who God is by looking at what His Word says and obeying it, the closer our relationship will become.

When we read God's Word, there are four primary benefits:
- The Bible helps guide us in life (Psalm 119:105).
- The Bible tells us what is right and wrong (Psalm 119:11).
- The Bible shows us the truth about humanity, and especially about ourselves (Hebrews 4:12).

- The Bible helps us understand God and His love for us (John 3:16-17).

 ## My Place in the Story

Abraham. Esther. Paul. You. What's odd about this list? Absolutely nothing. You and I are a part of the same story as Moses, David, and Mary. In a very real sense, we who are Christians continue to live out the still-unfolding Story of God. You see, God's Story, as found in the Bible, doesn't end with the Church in the Book of Acts; by our very lives, we are writing out new chapters every day. This happens as we read the biblical narratives, allowing them to shape us and our view of the world. Commit today to living out God's Story!

 ## Big Words

Doctrine—The teaching of a church on theological subjects, such as God, the Bible, and the end times. *Vital Beliefs* is a book about doctrine.

Inerrancy—The teaching that the writing of the Bible was so completely controlled by God that no errors of any kind appeared in the original manuscripts. Wesleyans do not hold to this teaching, but instead believe that God directed the writing of Scripture to the point that it is totally reliable in all matters of faith and salvation.

Inspiration—Refers to the Holy Spirit guiding the biblical writers so that they speak with God's authority.

Plenary Inspiration—The belief that the whole Bible was inspired by God.

Theology—The study of God and what He does.

Wesleyan Quadrilateral—A description of the four main resources Wesleyan theologians use to develop theological understandings.

 Did You Know?

- The Bible is broken into two sections. The Old Testament tells us what happened before Jesus came. The New Testament describes Jesus' life and impact on the Church.
- The Bible was written in three languages (Hebrew, Greek, and Aramaic) and contains several genres of writing, including history, poetry, and letters.
- The Bible was written over a period of about 1,500 years by more than 40 different people from three different continents.

These resources are Scripture, the traditional teachings of the Church, reason, and human experience. While Scripture is the foundational and most important basis for Wesleyan theology, Wesleyan theologians give more weight to human experience than do theologians in some other theological groups.

 Take It with You

All Scripture is God-breathed and is useful for teaching, rebuking, correcting and training in righteousness so that the man of God may be thoroughly equipped for every good work (2 Timothy 3:16-17).

 Giving It to God

Pray this prayer: *Father, forgive me for not spending time in Your Word. I want to know You better, and I realize I can do this as I read Your love letter to me. Inspire me to move from seeing reading the Bible as a "have to" and help it become a "want to." In Jesus' name. Amen.*

Dig Deeper

Here are some books that will be helpful if you want to do more studying on this important topic:

- *What the Bible Is All About,* NIV edition, by Henrietta Mears (Ventura, Calif.: Gospel Light, 1999). (083-072-4311)

   This book gives you a "big picture" view of the Bible, with summaries of every book of the Bible; key events in Scripture; and much more. Don't let its large size scare you, it is a very readable book.

- *Spending Time with God* by Mark Gilroy (Kansas City: Beacon Hill Press of Kansas City, 1999). (083-411-1977)

   A book that explains the need for personal devotions, and then shows you how to do it.

3

Sin

Something You're Born Into and Often Step In

 **Real Life**

It had been a tough week. As Kari lay on her bed, she softly wept as she thought about some of the things she had done that week. She had never meant to hurt anyone, but one thing had led to another, and before she knew it, it had snowballed out of control.

The week had started ordinary enough. On Monday at school, she was invited to a party on Friday night. Kari was excited, because she knew *all* the popular kids would be there. But she also knew her mom would never let her go. So Kari devised a plan. She told her mom she was going to spend Friday night at her best friend's house. Her mom agreed.

It was just a little lie, Kari thought. No one will get hurt.

Friday night, Kari joined her friends at the party. Soon the party was in full swing. Alcohol was freely available, and Kari felt she needed to drink to fit in. Drunk after a couple of beers, she thought she had never felt better. Everything seemed to be incredibly funny.

Then, while one partygoer was trying to show the others he could down a can of beer all at one time, the police walked in. Kari's heart immediately sank. She knew she was in big trouble.

> **To Quote**
>
> *Remember, there can be no little sin till we can find a little God.*
> —John Wesley, 18th-century English evangelist and the father of Wesleyan theology
>
> *All human sin seems so much worse in its consequences than in its intentions.*
> —Reinhold Niebuhr, 20th-century theologian

Her mom was called and had to come pick Kari up at the jail. Alternating expressions of fury and utter disappointment played back and forth on her mom's face like the slowly swinging pendulum of a clock. In addition to being charged with drinking as a minor, Kari was also being charged with vandalism. Some kids had destroyed one of the rooms in the house, and so everyone who had been present was being charged.

The tears flowed freely now. How could she have ever let herself get into such a mess?

Unfortunately, Kari's situation isn't uncommon. While her particular circumstances may be different, all of us have faced situations where we thought we could get by with a little disobedience only to find that it led to much bigger consequences.

Scripture refers to our disobedience to God as sin. This chapter will help you understand both what sin is and what its consequences are.

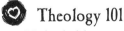 Your Life

1. How would you define "sin"?

2. Based on your definition of "sin," did you sin this week?

3. Do you think that sin has consequences? If so, what are they?

Theology 101

Nobody likes to talk about sin. Furthermore, nobody likes to admit that he or she has sinned. We all like to think we are basically good people. However, the Bible makes it clear that this is not the case. In Romans 3:23, the apostle Paul forever destroys that idea when he says, "For all have sinned and fall short of the glory of God." If this is so, then how did we all become sinners?

We believe sin came into the world because our original parents, Adam and Eve, blew it by disobeying God (see Genesis 3). Anytime we go against God, it's called sin. And because sin came into the world, we now know what it means to die. Sin is further broken down into two categories: (1) original sin or depravity and (2) personal sin.

Original sin is the corrupt nature we inherited from Adam and Eve. Just like we pick up some characteristics from our mom and dad, we inherited from our original parents original sin, which is also referred to as our sinful nature. Original sin has created in us an inborn tendency to do wrong. You might say it's something we are born into.

Personal sin is the wrong that you and I willfully choose to do even though we know it goes against God's will. An example is when you lie to your mom and dad. Lying is something you choose to do, even though you know it's wrong. However, don't mix personal sin up with involuntary shortcomings called faults, mistakes, failures, and fumbles. These are related to original sin.

Let me repeat: original sin is something we are born into; actual or personal sin is something we willingly choose to do.

Furthermore, when we speak of personal sin, we generally think of three distinct types. First, there is the **act of sin.** John Wesley defined a sin for which God holds people accountable as a willful transgression of the known will of God. Wesley believed people sin only when they miss the mark deliberately or when they choose the wrong mark to hit. Sin is not an accident or mistake we make. Sin is a deliberate choice to rebel against God's will. Examples of this would include: gossiping, cheating, lying, and stealing.

A second kind occurs not when we do something, but when we do nothing. These types of sin are commonly called **sins of omission.** This occurs when we know the right we should do and choose not to do it. James 4:17 says, "Anyone, then, who knows the good he ought to do and doesn't do it, sins." This could be a failure to speak the truth when we know it or to do something that we should have done.

Sin doesn't just have to be outward. **Sinful thoughts** can be just as devastating. This could be a wrong attitude, being jealous, hating somebody, or even coveting what someone else has. Jesus described such sins with this comment: "You have heard that it was said, 'Do not commit adultery.' But I tell you that anyone who looks at a woman lustfully has already committed adultery with her in his heart" (Matthew 5:27-28).

So, what are the consequences of sin? First, death entered the world because of Adam and Eve's sin. This is more than just a physical death. It is also a spiritual death.

If we die as sinful people, the Bible tells us there is a place called hell where we will forever be separated from all that is good and from God.

The second consequence of sin is that it destroys the relationship God intended us to have with Him. God created us in order to have a love relationship with Him. But sin puts a barrier between humanity and God. As a result, our relationship with God is hurt. If we do not turn away from sin, we will be separated from God both now and forever (the spiritual death mentioned above).

The third consequence of sin is that it destroys the relationships we have with each other. Sin affects every area of our lives: our mind, our emotions, and our actions. Because sin separates us from God, it stands to reason that our relationships with others will be affected as well. We see this all around us: racial hatred, murders, abuse, defamation, and oppression of others.

So why does a loving God need to punish us because of our sins? Because He is not only a God of love but also a holy God who is just. In the end, we will all stand before God where we "will have to give account to him who is ready to judge the living and the dead" (1 Peter 4:5).

🔍 Look It Up

1. For each of the following references, write down how the Bible describes sin:
   Romans 14:23; 1 John 3:4; James 4:17; 1 John 5:17

   Sin is Lawlessness, breaking the law

2. Read Genesis 3. List all the consequences that Adam and Eve faced because of their sin.

3. Revelation 20:11-15 tells us what will happen when we stand before God. What will be the result of those who stand before God as sinners?

 ## Why Should I Care?

Watch your local news. Chances are you will see some of the results of sin: wrongs suffered, painful consequences, broken relationships. The consequences of sin affect not only you but others as well. Sin is not just a personal matter; it always impacts the community at large in some way.

But the most important reason why you should care about sin is that it separates you from God. This separation doesn't just occur after death. It occurs now. Because God is holy and can't stand the presence of sin, He cannot have a relationship with sinful people. Trying to live without God is to live only half a life.

So what can we do about sin? We have to recognize we can't overcome sin by ourselves. Sin is powerful, but there is One who is more powerful. We'll discover what God's answer to sin is in the next chapter.

 ## My Place in the Story

God invites all of us to enter into His Story. But there are many false stories at work that keep people from entering into the Story. These false stories often promise much but fail to deliver in the end. The common thread in all these false stories is sin. Sin breeds brokenness—both in creation and in our relations. The Story of God is primarily concerned with healing this brokenness, which is the topic of the next chapter.

 ### Did You Know?

Genesis 3 gives us three steps in sinning:
1. Doubt God's Word ("Did God really say . . . ?")
2. Disbelieve God's Word ("You will not surely die.")
3. Disobey God's Word (By eating the fruit of the tree)

 ## Big Words

Depravity—A person's state as a result of original sin. This person seeks

31

the opposite of what God intended for us and does not desire any relationship with God or with good.

Image—Likeness; being like someone else. When used in reference to the image of God, it means that we are like God because we have a free will.

Original Sin—A phrase with a twofold meaning. It refers to the first sin committed by Adam and Eve. It also refers to the tendency of humanity to sinfully rebel against God.

Sinful Nature—The sin in our spirit that came from Adam and Eve. It is this sin that causes us to sin and rebel against God.

Sins—The actions and thoughts of people done willingly and knowingly against God's will.

 ## Giving It to God

Pray this prayer: *Father, I know that I am a sinner. I recognize that my sins have affected not only my relationship with You but with others as well. I'm tired of dealing with sin's consequences. Help me stay away from sin and draw closer to You. Amen.*

 Take It with You

But your iniquities have separated you from your God; your sins have hidden his face from you (Isaiah 59:2).

 ## Dig Deeper

Here are some books that will be helpful if you want to do more studying on this important topic:

- *Coffee Shop Theology* by Frank Moore (Kansas City: Beacon Hill Press of Kansas City, 1998). (083-411-7320)

    Chapters 18 and 19 of this book give a good overview of sin and its destructive power.

- *A Right Conception of Sin* by Richard S. Taylor (Kansas City: Beacon Hill Press of Kansas City, 1945). (083-410-1394)

    Taylor takes a comprehensive look at sin according to the Bible.

4

Salvation
The First Step

 **Real Life**

Miguel was confused. He had come to the lock-in because his friend had promised it would be a lot of fun. And the truth was, it had been fun. At least until now. He hadn't realized that he would have to sit and listen to some preacher. *Boy, what a waste of time,* thought Miguel. But as he sat listening to the speaker talk about having a relationship with God, something inside him reacted. For reasons that he didn't completely understand, Miguel knew that this was what he needed. While he generally thought of himself as a good guy, he also recognized that there were some areas of his life he didn't like very much.

 To Quote

Grace means that there is nothing we can do to make God love us more. . . . And grace means that there is nothing we can do to make God love us less.
—Philip Yancey, 20th-century writer

True believers are saved from inward and outward sin by faith.
—John Wesley, 18th-century English evangelist and the father of Wesleyan theology

The speaker continued on, saying that Jesus Christ had come to earth for one purpose—to save us from our sins. He quoted a verse from the Bible: "But God demonstrates his own love for us in this: While we were still sinners, Christ died for us" (Romans 5:8).

Wow, thought Miguel. *Jesus came to earth to die just for me? But why?*

As if he was reading Miguel's mind, the speaker explained, "Jesus came to die for us so that we could have life. Jesus loves us and desires to have a relationship with us."

A relationship with me, Miguel wondered. *No way. If Jesus is as pure and holy as this guy says, there is no way He would want a relationship with me.*

"And the best part about this," continued the speaker, "is that it doesn't matter how many sins you may have committed or how bad you think you are. Jesus Christ still loves you and wants to make His home in your heart. If you desire to have Jesus forgive you of your sins, then I invite you to come forward tonight and ask Him to do that."

Miguel immediately got out of his seat. If what this speaker said was true, Miguel knew that he needed it. Kneeling at a makeshift altar up front, Miguel was met by the speaker he had been listening to. He led Miguel in a prayer, asking God's forgiveness for his sins, and inviting God to come live in his heart.

When Miguel finished praying, he felt different. Nothing had changed outwardly, but inside he knew something was different. God had met him, and somehow Miguel knew he would never be the same again.

As we discovered in the last chapter, sin can be pretty powerful. But as Miguel discovered, God is more powerful. Only He can defeat sin in our lives. Let's examine what it means to accept Jesus Christ as our Savior in this chapter.

Your Life

1. Give your own definition of what you think "salvation" means.

2. What are some reasons people give for not accepting Jesus as their Savior?

3. Have you accepted Jesus as your Savior? If so, why? If not, why not?

🎨 Theology 101

When God created us, He gave us a gift that no other creature received—free will. Basically, having a free will means that God gave us the ability to make our own choices. This includes having the ability to choose not to love God.

Why would God give us this choice, knowing that we would abuse it, resulting in sin? Because God wanted His love returned freely. By giving us a choice, God knew if we chose to love Him, it would be a genuine, absolute, undiluted love. God wanted a relationship with us so much He gave us the choice to not love Him.

But as we saw in the last chapter, humanity abused that freedom. Sin became rampant, so much so that at one point God decided to start over (see Genesis 6:5-7). But even after this new start, sin once again flourished. God knew humanity needed a way out, and so He provided one.

God set up a system whereby the people could ask forgiveness for their sins by offering an animal in sacrifice. They would have to choose a spotless animal, one free of any defects, and take it to the Temple. There the priest would symbolically pray the sins of the person onto the animal. Then the priest would kill the animal and pour out its blood before God as a sin offering. God would see this act of obedience and repentance and would in turn forgive the person's sin. Why did God require His people to kill an animal to receive forgiveness? God wanted them to know that sin is serious, so serious that it takes a life to pay for it.

However, this system of getting forgiveness was only temporary. From the beginning of time, God had been working on a plan to reclaim the entire human race. This plan involved sending His Son, Jesus Christ, to earth in order to die so we could be saved. You see, before we ever knew or cared, God showed His great love for us in giving Christ to die, that we might be saved from wrath through Him (Romans 5:8-9). Jesus came as the once-and-for-all, final, complete sacrifice for our sin. That's why Jesus is called the Lamb of God. By shedding His blood for us, He offered us a new chance at life.

But the truth is if Jesus had just died that would have been the end of the story. While Jesus' death provided payment for our sins, it was His rising from the dead three days later that gives us hope for the future.

How does the death and resurrection of Jesus make a difference? First, by forgiving us of our sins. Christ's shed blood covers our hearts, making our spirits pure again. When He forgives our sins, God removes them as far from us as the east is from the west (Psalm 103:11-12).

Second, our relationship with God is restored. The barrier sin erected between God and us is destroyed. In fact, when Jesus died on the Cross, the Bible tells us a large, heavy curtain in the Temple was ripped in two, from top to bottom. This curtain separated the place where only the high priest annually went to make a symbolic sacrifice for the sins of the people. The ripping of the curtain symbolized that a new way had emerged for us to approach God and receive forgiveness for our sins.

Third, you are given membership in God's family. You are a daughter or son of God. And God is your Father. This family relationship extends to all those who have accepted Jesus Christ as their Savior. You are a brother or sister to those who call themselves Christian.

Last, Christ's death saves us from the punishment of sin and assures us a place in heaven with Him forever.

So what happens when we confess our sins and tell God we're sorry? We commonly say there are three things that occur.

- **Justification** is the act by which God reconciles people to himself. It is God's act in pardoning the guilt and setting aside the penalty of all our sins and accepting us as righteous through faith in Christ.

- **Regeneration** is the act by which God gives us new life. It is the renewal of our fallen natures whereby we become alive spiritually and are made capable of faith, love, and obedience.

- **Adoption** is the act by which God makes us His children. Justification and adoption are what God does *for* us; regeneration is what He does *in* us. All three of these acts happen at the same time.

The best thing about God's plan of salvation is it's free! There is nothing we can do to earn it. We simply have to accept it as the free gift God intended it to be.

Look It Up

1. According to John 14:6, what is the only way we can come to God and receive salvation?

2. Look up Hebrews 9:11 and 10:10. What were the two roles Christ assumed in His death on the Cross?

3. According to 2 Corinthians 5:17, what is the result when we accept Christ as our Savior?

 # Why Should I Care?

Brennan Manning, in his book *The Ragamuffin Gospel*, tells about a woman who was reported to have had visions of Jesus.[1] A religious man decided to check her out.

"It is true, ma'am, that you have visions of Jesus?" asked the cleric.

"Yes," the woman replied simply.

The man told her to ask Jesus, next time He appeared, to tell her the sins that the man had recently confessed.

"You actually want me to ask Jesus to tell me the sins of your past?" she asked.

"Exactly. Please call me if anything happens."

Ten days later the woman called, saying Jesus had appeared. The man rushed to her house.

"I asked Jesus to tell me the sin you confessed," the woman said.

The man leaned forward with anticipation. His eyes narrowed. "What did Jesus say?"

She took his hands and gazed deep into his eyes. "These are His exact words: 'I CAN'T REMEMBER.'"

To be blunt, if we die with sin in our life, the Bible says that we will spend eternity in hell. But, if we confess our sins to Jesus Christ, we can have the same assurance that the lady gave to the skeptic.

We can know that our sins have not only been forgiven but forgotten as well. That is the greatest news we can have not only because it gives us a relationship with Jesus now but also because we can know that when we die, we will go to heaven to live with Him forever.

Have you asked Jesus Christ into your life? If not, now is the best time to experience His forgiveness and love. You see, as great as God's free gift of salvation is, it doesn't do us any good until we accept it. If you wish to do this, pray the prayer found in the *Give It to God* section. If you have accepted Jesus, rejoice in the fact that He has forgiven you and walks with you daily.

 ## My Place in the Story

Salvation is the primary theme of the Story of God. In fact, this Story is all about a God who so desperately loved us that He was willing to do whatever it took to cleanse us from sin and restore us to himself—even to die for us. Our response to this act of love is to claim our rightful place in the Story, and to invite others to find their place as well.

 ## Big Words

Atonement—How God forgives sin through the sacrifice of His Son, Jesus Christ.

Born Again—A term describing those who receive a new life when they are saved.

Faith—A response of trust in God in which a Christian not only believes in God but acts on that belief in obedience.

Forgiveness—The act that makes a person free from guilt and blame for doing wrong.

Grace—The undeserved mercy of God extended to sinners.

Incarnation—A term used to describe the act of God becoming human in the form of Jesus by taking upon himself a human body.

Prevenient Grace—The love of God that reaches out to all people

 Did You Know?

In some countries, to be called a Christian is to literally have a death sentence placed on your head. Those who live in those countries know accepting Christ is certain death, and yet they still do it. What does this tell you about the difference Christ makes in a person's life?

before conversion, which enables them to accept Christ as their Lord and Savior.

Redemption—Jesus Christ paid the price to set us free from our slavery to sin with His death at Calvary. However, it is still up to each individual to choose to accept this freedom.

Repentance—The act of asking God to forgive us of our sins and our turning away from sin and toward obedience to God.

Salvation—The act by which God saves His people from their sins.

 ## Giving It to God

Pray this prayer—*Gracious God, I know I'm a sinner. Like Adam and Eve, I have chosen to rebel against You. But now I ask that You would forgive me for my sins and cleanse my heart. Come into my life and be my Savior. I pledge to be obedient to Your will. In Jesus' name. Amen.*

Take It with You

If we confess our sins, he is faithful and just and will forgive us our sins and purify us from all unrighteousness (1 John 1:9).

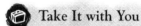 ## Dig Deeper

Here are some books that will be helpful if you want to do more studying on this important topic:

- *In the Grip of Grace* by Max Lucado (Dallas: Word, 1996). (084-991-1435)

    One of the best descriptions of God and His grace that I know of.

- *Life of the Beloved* by Henri Nouwen (New York: Crossroad, 1982). (082-451-1840)

    This book describes for us the intimate relationship that God desires with each of us.

5

Sanctification
The Second Step

 Real Life

"It's just that I'm tired of always screwing up, and then having to ask God for forgiveness again," moaned Brad. "In fact, it seems that most of my time with God is spent confessing the same sins over and over. I love God and want to serve Him, but I just can't seem to make any progress spiritually."

Susie, Brad's youth pastor, listened carefully. It had been just six months since Brad gave his heart to Jesus Christ and had become a Christian. Since then, he'd become actively involved in the church and youth group. Brad was a popular person at school, all-state in wrestling, and therefore a lot of others had noticed the change as well. Susie knew Brad really tried to set an example for his friends of what a Christian was like, but she also knew that sometimes he messed up. She knew that Brad needed to take the next step in his spiritual walk, and so she tried to think how to explain this to Brad.

"Brad, I know what you're saying," Susie responded. "I felt that way once before as well. In fact, all Christians eventually come to the place where they realize they can't make it in their own strength."

 To Quote

But we must love God, before we can be holy at all; this being the root of all holiness.
—John Wesley, 18th-century English evangelist and the father of Wesleyan theology

I cannot, by direct moral effort, give myself new motives. After the first few steps in the Christian life we realise that everything which really needs to be done in our souls can be done only by God.
—C. S. Lewis, 20th-century author

This caught Brad's attention. "If we don't have the strength to make it, then how can we ever make it as Christians?"

"The truth is, we can't. At least not on our own. You see, you and I have a disadvantage in trying to live the Christian life. Because of Adam and Eve's sin, all of humanity is under a curse. We are all born with a predisposition to sin. It's not natural for us to want to serve God; instead we want to serve only ourselves. This predisposition to sin, what we call original sin, makes it impossible for us to live for Christ by ourselves."

Brad interrupted. "But there are plenty of Christians I know who seem to be able to live free of sin and full of love for God. How do they do it?"

Susie continued. "They've recognized that if they are going to gain any consistency in their lives, they need the power of the Holy Spirit."

"What does the Holy Spirit do?" asked Brad.

"He's able to remove our desire to sin, and to give us a greater love for God and others. But He can only do it if we are willing to give Him total control of our lives."

As Susie looked at Brad, she could see he was struggling to understand this. She wondered how she could better explain it. Brad's school letterman jacket with all of its medals and patches caught her eye, reminding her of his athletic abilities.

"Brad, let me see if I can put this in terms you can understand. As the reigning state wrestling champion, you are used to being in control on the mat. Since you have never been pinned, you've never experienced what it is like for someone else to be in charge. Well, the only way to remove our sinful nature is to allow the Holy Spirit to be in control of every area of our life. In your language, the Holy Spirit pins us. When we give Him control, He not only removes the sinful nature but also gives us the power we need to resist sin."

Brad had been listening intently. What Susie said made sense. And so, sitting there in the booth at the restaurant, Brad gave the Holy Spirit control of his life.

Brad recognized that he needed something more in his life. What Brad experienced that day is called entire sanctification. Let's examine what it's all about.

💿 Your Life

1. On the scale below, rank where you feel you are spiritually.

Separated from God	Relationship Started	Growth Happening	Solidly Connected

2. Why do you think it is so hard to live a consistent Christian life?

3. What do you most need from God in order to live faithfully for Him?

♡ Theology 101

When we accept Jesus Christ as our Savior, we eagerly desire to serve Christ and to learn more about Him. We want to share with others what God has done in our life. And so begins a wonderful journey.

But as we grow in grace we become increasingly sensitive to God's will and begin to recognize when our actions and attitudes do not measure up to God's will. We also perceive that we do not have the power by ourselves to resist the temptations we face. Try as we might, we're not always able to do what is right and avoid what's wrong. Paul expressed this vividly when he said,

> I know that nothing good lives in me, that is, in my sinful nature. For I have the desire to do what is good, but I cannot carry it out. For what I do is not the good I want to do; no, the evil I do not want to do—this I keep on doing *(Romans 7:18-19)*.

If this is the case, what can be done about this?

Simply put, we need to be entirely sanctified. Maybe you will understand it better if we conduct a small question-and-answer session.

What does it mean to be sanctified? Basically it means the total, lifelong process of becoming holy.

What does it mean to be holy? *Holy* describes the perfection and unity of God that are His alone. When used to describe us, it means we have been set apart for God's use.

Why should I become holy? Because God commands it (Leviticus 19:2). As a disciple, you are called to imitate God in all you do. Since God is holy, you should also be a holy person.

Am I not holy at salvation? In a word, no. In salvation you are saved from your sins, and you start a new relationship with God. It is at this point that the Holy Spirit (the third person of the Trinity) is also given to you to act as your guide. This is called initial sanctification.

How do I become holy? By confessing your need to God and surrendering yourself to His will. When you do this, God fills you with His Holy Spirit. God cleanses the sinful nature (original sin) from your heart. The Holy Spirit then gives you power to live for and serve God. This is the act of entire sanctification—you surrender yourself to God, and He sanctifies you.

What's the result of this entire sanctification? When God cleanses the sinful nature, He removes the desire to sin. He makes the person's heart pure and holy. The person receives power to serve God with all of his or her heart and to witness. Prior to this experience, most people do not understand or have access to the power and the joy that the Holy Spirit brings.

When does entire sanctification happen? At the moment you surrender yourself to God entirely. Sanctification involves both a crisis (the cleansing of our sinful nature) and a process (continued growth). Entire sanctification does not end growth. Instead, it promotes it. It's a beginning point—a vital step in the lifelong process of being made more like Christ.

Let's illustrate what has been said. Compare your life to driving a car. Before you are saved, you are the only person in the car. You go where you want when you want. You control the car.

When you are saved, you invite God into the car. You and God have a great time cruising through life, enjoying each other's company. But every so often, you make a stop at a place that's harmful to you (that is, to your spiritual life). You sense God doesn't want to be there and doesn't want you to be there. God begins to speak to you about where you drive your car. God eventually asks you to let Him drive.

At this point, you resist. It has been great having God along for the ride and all, but allowing God to drive means you would have to give up control. No longer would you be able to choose where you want to go and when you want to go. You're just not sure you want to do that.

God begins to speak again. He points out that He has some incredible places He wants to take you, but you can only get there if you allow God to drive.

You ask, "But can't we just keep things like they were? You know, you and I just enjoying life, with me still driving?"

But God is firm. "When you first invited Me in the car, I came willingly. You stated then that you were tired of the places you were going, and you wanted a navigator, someone who could help you get where you needed to go. But lately, you've been ignoring My directions, going to places that aren't on My map. Therefore, if you are serious about wanting to go where you need to go, I have to be more than just your navigator. I also need to be the driver. Only then can I help you get to your final destination."

You're scared. When you first invited God in, you hadn't expected to have to give up control. But you're also tired. You really don't want to stop at those bad places along the way, but sometimes you just can't seem to stop yourself. As you think about it, you realize God has been a great navigator. You know He's always had your best interests in mind and has never gotten you lost. And so, pulling over by the side of the road, you get out and hand God the keys. "OK, God. You drive," you say.

Smiling, God takes the keys. The two of you get back in the car, and God puts it in gear. As you take off, you put your head back against the headrest, sighing in contentment. Somehow, you sense you made the right decision.

🔍 Look It Up

1. According to Leviticus 11:45, why were the people of Israel to be holy?

2. According to Acts 1:8 and 15:8-9, what are the two lasting results of sanctification?

3. According to 1 Thessalonians 5:12-24, what does Paul say the sanctified life should be like?

 ## Why Should I Care?

Too often we simply see sanctification as something to be obtained. We want God to cleanse our heart of original sin and to give us power. The truth is, we don't like the idea of giving up control. The question with sanctification is not, "How much of God do I have?" Instead it should be, "How much of me does God have?"

You see, as you continue to grow in Christ, you realize quickly that God has given you all of himself. You enjoy the intimacy He offers and lean on Him in times of trouble. But the closer the two of you become, the more you begin to realize your attitudes and actions don't always match what God wants. In fact, the closer the two of you get, the more you understand how unlike God you really are.

It's at this point God begins to talk to you. He reminds you that at salvation He gave you all of himself. He held nothing back. Now, if this relationship is to go forward, you must do the same—you must give all of yourself to God.

The reason sanctification is so important is because it's the only way we can continue to grow in our relationship with God. When we get to the point that our sin nature is keeping us from fully serving God, we have to make the decision. Are we content to just live a nominal Christian life that kind of gets by, or do we want the full, rich Christian life God has promised us? The only way to get the latter is to be entirely sanctified.

So how do you become sanctified? There are four steps we need to follow:

1. Believe that it's the will of God (1 Thessalonians 4:3).

2. Surrender your life to God (Romans 6:19).

3. Separate yourself to God (2 Corinthians 6:17; 7:1).

4. Trust God to cleanse your heart of all sin (1 John 1:9).

If you have not been entirely sanctified, there is no better time than right now. Follow the four steps, and allow God to cleanse your heart and empower you for His service.

 ## My Place in the Story

After we have been in the Story for a period of time, we recognize that God demands much of those who live according to the Story. In essence, participation in the Story of God asks that we begin orienting ourselves solely toward God. The problem is most of us try to make God fit our lives. But the Story of God requires us to turn our lives over to God and allow Him to fit our lives into His Story. When this happens, we move from sinful, self-centeredness to Christ-centeredness. And that's what living the Story is all about.

 ## Big Words

Christian Perfection—A phrase meaning the same as entire sanctification. It means to be made perfect in love toward God and humanity. This is not a perfection of thoughts and actions, but a perfection of relationship to God.

Consecration—The act Christians make by setting themselves apart to God and His service.

Entire Sanctification—A term to describe the act of God in which He cleanses the sinful nature from believers, makes them holy in motives and actions, and gives them power to live a holy life.

Holiness—Complete commitment to God. Can also serve as a synonym for entire sanctification.

Initial Sanctification—A term to show that a person begins having a holy relationship with God at conversion.

Perfect Love—Wholehearted love for God and others. Another

Did You Know?

Holiness is too often confused with obeying lots of rules. But that's not what holiness is. Holiness is ultimately a relationship between you and God. While it is concerned with how we act, it sees our actions as the product of our relationship with God. In other words, holiness describes the love story between us and God.

47

term used for entire sanctification.

 ## Giving It to God

Pray this prayer: *Gracious God, I recognize that I need more of You in my life. I'm tired of trying to overcome sin by my own power. I need Your power in my life. I ask You to cleanse my heart of inbred sin, fill me with Your Spirit, and supply me with Your power. In Your holy name I pray. Amen.*

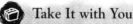 ### Take It with You

May God himself, the God of peace, sanctify you through and through. May your whole spirit, soul and body be kept blameless at the coming of our Lord Jesus Christ. The one who calls you is faithful and he will do it (1 Thessalonians 5:23-24).

Dig Deeper

Here are some books that will be helpful if you want to do more studying on this important topic:

- *Holiness for Ordinary People* by Keith Drury (Marion, Ind.: Wesleyan Publishing House, 1983). (089-827-1320)

  This book is written on a level that most teens can easily understand.

- *The House: A Parable on Entire Sanctification* (Kansas City: WordAction Publishing, 1990). (VE-750)

6

Evil

Why Does It Seem God Is Always Losing?

 Real Life

Lauryn slumped in her seat. It seemed like her mom had been in the doctor's office forever. How much longer would she be?

Lauryn had not wanted to be there, but for some reason her mom had asked her to come with her. As she sat there waiting impatiently, Lauryn began recalling the last two years of her life.

Things had become much tougher ever since her dad had died in the car accident. Even now, after two years, it still caused her to get emo-

To Quote

The mystery of evil is the source of our greatest vulnerability as believers.
—Robert McAfee Brown, 20th-century theologian

For this purpose the Son of God was manifested, that he might destroy the works of the devil.
—John Wesley, 18th-century English evangelist and the father of Wesleyan theology

tional. She had struggled mightily in her Christian faith because of her father's death, wondering how a good God could do something like that. Her pastor had tried to help her during that tough time, but he just didn't seem to understand what Lauryn was going through.

Fortunately, with the help of her mom and her closest friends, Lauryn had come through those dark days. She had reclaimed her faith in Christ and was active once again in the church, particularly in her youth group. She felt like she had been through the worst Satan could throw at her, and now she would be able to make it.

Just then, a nurse came out and asked Lauryn if she would come back to see her mother. Curious, Lauryn agreed. As she entered the doctor's office, Lauryn could see her mother had been crying. "What's wrong?" Lauryn asked.

Solemnly, the doctor looked Lauryn in the eye and said, "Lauryn, I'm afraid I've got some bad news. Your mother has cancer, and she only has about six months to live."

Lauryn's head started spinning. Cancer. It couldn't be. She had already lost her dad, and now this doctor was telling her she was going to lose her mom as well. Why was this happening to her? Hadn't she already been through enough? And where was God? Why was He allowing this to happen?

As Lauryn sat there, angry and confused, she decided at that moment if God would allow this to happen, then He wasn't a God she wanted to serve.

Have you ever felt like Lauryn? Maybe your circumstances weren't nearly as devastating, and maybe you never really came to the point of giving up your faith. But the simple truth is we are all bothered by the question, "Why is it that evil always seems to win, and God always seems to lose?" Let's explore that question in this chapter.

 Your Life

1. Who is more powerful—God or Satan? Why?

2. Why do you think bad things happen to Christians?

3. Think about a situation in your own life where something tragic occurred. Do you think that God could have prevented it? Why, or why not?

♥ Theology 101

Coming to grips with tragedy is never easy. But for Christians it often seems doubly difficult. Not only do we have to deal with the tragedy itself, but we have to figure out how this tragedy fits into our beliefs about God.

So how do we deal with this problem of evil? Well, for starters, we must understand where evil comes from. Evil began as a choice made by an angel (commonly referred to as Lucifer) to rebel against God. He chose to misuse his freedom (his free will) by seeking to be equal with God. As we saw in the chapter on sin, the misuse of our free will is where sin originates.

Because of his act of rebellion, Lucifer and those who followed him were cast out of heaven by God (Isaiah 14:12-17). Lucifer, now known as Satan, sought to undermine God in every way possible. Because he knew what his end would be (check the chapter on Last Things—it's next), he sought to destroy every good thing God had made.

When Adam and Eve came along, Satan saw the perfect opportunity to put a serious crimp into God's plans. And so, using the same temptation he had himself succumbed to, Satan tempted Adam and Eve. And as we know, they gave in as well.

Now before we blame Satan entirely, let me interject this. Satan is *not* the cause of our sinning. We can never say when we choose to give in to temptation, "The devil made me do it." To do so would be to excuse ourselves from all personal responsibility for our sinning. No, the Bible doesn't let us "off the hook" that easily. However, while Satan certainly tempts us, and his power is great, we have to remember that with God's strength we can resist temptation because "the one who is in you is greater than the one who is in the world" (1 John 4:4).

As we discovered in the chapter on sanctification, Adam and Eve's sin affected all of humanity, giving us a sinful nature that does not seek God or His best. Instead, this sinful nature is selfish and seeks only what is best for the self. Therefore, we do not seek the good of others, and if we think it will benefit us, we will even seek their harm. This is commonly referred to as moral evil. Think about the effects of sinful natures at work today: murder, rape, a drunk driver hitting a kid, stealing a car. All of these are the result of the sinful nature seeking to please itself.

Moral evil refers both to individual choice (as seen above) as well as to the choices made by social, economic, or political organizations or practices. When it is corporate in nature, it's referred to as systemic evil. Some examples of systemic evil would include: making legal the practice of abortion and homosexuality; allowing racism to be practiced because a society simply ignores the problem; and killing systematically one group of people for no other reason than that they are different.

Furthermore, as a result of Adam and Eve's sin, the world in which we live was cursed (Genesis 3:17-19). This curse brought about what we refer to as natural evil. Natural evil is broken into two categories: destructive forces of nature (i.e., earthquakes and tornadoes) and destructive forces of diseases (i.e., cancer and diabetes).

Evil abounds. We see it everywhere we look. And from the Genesis story of creation, we understand the causes of some evil can be attributed to our free will. God loved us so much He was willing to give us free will, even though He knew that free will has potential for both good and evil. But in order for our love for God to be genuine, there was no other way.

Still, we struggle when evil occurs and it seems like God could have stopped it from happening. The simple fact is, we don't always understand why God seems to allow evil to occur. And furthermore, we never will, at least not in this lifetime. So what do we do?

In his insightful book *The Problem of Pain*, C. S. Lewis acknowledged that Christians may never be able to resolve this question of why evil occurs, but they still know how to pray, how to seek God's comfort and assurance, how to resist and protest the forces of evil, and how to give one another encouragement in times of trouble and pain.[1] This is the Christian response to suffering because it has always been God's response to the suffering of His people.

You see, God never promised us a life free from evil and suffering. But He did promise He would be with us when we face it. The day Jesus was crucified on a cross, He took upon himself all the evil the world had to offer. He did this so He could identify with what we face and how we suffer. We can never again say God doesn't understand because He does. And because He understands, He is present with us, working unfailingly to overcome evil.

As good as this news is, there is even greater news. God not only identifies with our suffering but has once and for all conquered evil! On Easter Sunday morning, Jesus Christ took the worst that Satan could throw at Him and came through it victorious!

Yes, we will still experience pain and sorrow while we are here on this earth. But we can rest in the assurance not only that God is with us when evil strikes but also that He has already defeated Satan and death. When we don't understand why, we need to trust in God. After all, He is the One who has already won the war over evil.

 ## Look It Up

1. What does Paul mean in 2 Corinthians 11:14 when he says that Satan "masquerades as an angel of light"? What are some examples of this?

2. According to John 8:44, what is Satan's native language? How does he use this language against Christians?

3. In Genesis 3:17-19, what are the results of humanity's abuse of our free will? How is this evident today?

4. According to 1 John 4:4, what promise can we hold to regarding the presence of evil? Why is this promise so important?

 ## Big Words

Satan—The name of the devil who is the enemy of God. He is the most powerful of the evil spirits.

Systemic Evil—The building of systems that do not honor God. It is a philosophy of life that opposes God's ways. It is sinful practices that seem normal.

 # Why Should I Care?

When we face suffering and evil, none of us wants to go through it alone. We all desire for others to come alongside us and, by their presence, give us hope.

That is, in effect, what Jesus does. But the hope He offers is much more than just optimism or feeling happy for a few days. The hope He offers is one that assures us in the end all will be for our good. This hope says He has already won the final battle over evil. And it's a hope promising that He will be present when we face the evils of our day. While the pain of evil doesn't lessen, our Hope gives us a place where we can stand.

Non-Christians have to face these evils without this hope. Even their friends can't give them the hope they need because they, too, are powerless against such incredible forces of evil.

 Did You Know?

Often, when we face evil, we tend to direct our anger against God. And, the truth of the matter is, that is OK. God isn't bothered by our honest questions. He wants us to be completely open and honest with Him regarding how we are feeling and that we don't understand why this evil has occurred. The Psalms are full of instances where the psalmist questions God's actions (or inaction) and releases his anger upon God. And in those cases, God responds, not in anger, but in love. We truly serve a merciful God.

The next time you have to endure the evils of this world, don't do it in your own power. Trust in the One who has already defeated evil once and for all. God may not take the evil away, but He will walk with us as we go through it. That's the sign of a true Friend.

 # My Place in the Story

Those who are a part of the Story of God are not exempt from facing evil. They will have to endure the same heartaches and suffering as non-Christians. But the one advantage we who live in the Story have is that we don't face these things alone. We understand we are a part of a community of faith willing to stand beside us as fellow participants in the Story. And most importantly, the author of the Story himself, Jesus Christ, chooses to stand with us. What an encouraging thought!

Giving It to God

Pray this prayer: *Father, I know I live in an evil world, and I don't always understand why evil things happen. And I admit that at times I have to question why You don't stop this great evil from happening. But I also know You are God, and Your wisdom is far greater than mine. Help me, when evil comes, not to blame You but to trust You, not to give up but to give it to You. And most of all, let me always remember Your great response to this problem of evil—the giving of Your own Son to die for me. In Your name I pray. Amen.*

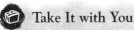 Take It with You

Be self-controlled and alert. Your enemy the devil prowls around like a roaring lion looking for someone to devour. Resist him, standing firm in your faith, because you know that your brothers throughout the world are going through the same kind of sufferings (1 Peter 5:8-9).

Dig Deeper

Here is a book that will be helpful if you want to do more studying on this important topic:

- *If God Is God, Then Why?* by Al Truesdale (Kansas City: Beacon Hill Press of Kansas City, 1997). (083-411-6316)

   In a series of letters between an uncle and his niece, they attempt to make sense of the tragedy of the Oklahoma City bombing. A superb book on how we respond to evil.

7

Last Things
The Second Coming, Heaven, and Hell

 **Real Life**

"Man, that was cool," said Khalid. "I just love the X-Files. You know, I think this show has a lot of truth to it. I don't know exactly how things will end, but who's to say that we won't all be taken up by a huge flying saucer someday?"

Stephon had also enjoyed the X-Files episode they had just watched. But he struggled with what Khalid said. Stephon didn't really believe there were aliens who would come one day and take everyone with them. But he had often wondered what would happen at the end of time. He thought

 To Quote

Why should anyone be shattered by the thought of hell? It is not compulsory for anyone to go there.

—Thomas Merton, 20th-century philosopher, author, and monk

The Son of God, manifested in the clouds of heaven, shall destroy this last work of the devil.

—John Wesley, 18th-century English evangelist and the father of Wesleyan theology

back to what his pastor had preached on that past Sunday. He had stated that Jesus Christ would return one day and would judge all of humanity for their sins. For those whose lives are full of sin, they will receive the punishment for their sin—hell. When his pastor had first said that, Stephon had gotten a sick feeling in his stomach. He had certainly committed a lot of sins in his life. Was he bound for hell? But that sick feeling quickly dissipated when his pastor went on to say, "But for those who have accepted Jesus Christ as their Savior, they will go to heaven."

Stephon's thoughts were interrupted by Khalid. "What do you think?" Khalid asked. "What happens when we die?"

Stephon breathed a quick prayer. Khalid was one of his best friends, but he wasn't a Christian. Would he really understand what Stephon believed? Or would he make fun of him because he believed Jesus Christ would come back to judge all people? *Dear Lord, help me to be honest with Khalid about what I believe concerning Your coming again. Open his heart to what I say, and may this be another opportunity to help him understand who You are.*

Stephon smiled at his friend. "OK, here's what I believe . . ."

There are a lot of people like Khalid, who are struggling to make sense of what will happen in the last days. You may even be one of them. Unfortunately, there are a lot of people out there spreading some warped ideas. In this chapter, we will try to answer some of your questions as we focus on what we definitely know will happen during the last days.

Your Life

1. Describe what you think heaven will be like.

2. Describe what you think hell will be like.

3. If you were to die right now, where do you think you would go? Why?

Theology 101

The Bible is clear about two things: all human beings will die a physical death (Hebrews 9:27) and the world as we know it will end someday. These two events are a part of the study of last things, what theologians refer to as eschatology.

While we recognize death is inevitable, we also recognize one of the central truths of the Christian faith is the promise that death is not the end. We believe that after death, we will be resurrected (Matthew 22:23 ff.). The resurrection of Jesus Christ is the hope and model for our own resurrection. Without His resurrection, death would be terrifying because death would truly signify the end. But the Bible teaches that on resurrection day, our bodies will be resurrected as a new and glorious body free of any imperfections (1 Corinthians 15). While this body will be a spiritual body, much like Christ's resurrected body, we will recognize each other and maintain our personal identity.

When will this happen? When Christ comes again. The Bible makes it plain that, just as Christ came once before as a baby, He will again, this time with power and glory. When Christ returns, He will judge all people. This is commonly referred to as the Final Judgment (also called the Great White Throne Judgment).

At this judgment, Christ will judge everyone who has ever lived. All those who have died will be raised, and they, along with everyone who is still alive, will be required to stand before God. Each of us will be judged for our deeds (both good and bad) in this life. God will also judge us according to our relationship with Jesus. If we have accepted Jesus as our Savior, we have God's forgiveness and will go to live with God forever. However, if we have not asked Jesus to forgive our sins, then we will spend eternity in hell. Let's examine each of these in more detail.

What we know about heaven comes from two primary biblical sources: the Book of Revelation (see especially chapter 21), and what Jesus told us. A lot of the information from Revelation is hard to understand because the apostle John was writing symbolically. For instance, he writes that heaven is a cube. When heaven is described as a cube, we can't take this literally. In ancient literature a cube with equal dimensions was considered perfect. Therefore, what John was trying to convey to us is that heaven is a place of perfection.

When Jesus talked about heaven, His descriptions of heaven were not based on theory but from personal experience. When Jesus describes heaven He uses some great imagery: plenty of room for everyone (John 14:2); unity and harmony will be the norm (17:20-22); a loving Father is waiting at the door for our arrival (Luke 15:20). Most importantly, He tells us it's the place where God lives

(Matthew 6:9). Communion with God is the essence of heaven. This alone should make us want to go there.

Heaven will be significant because of what isn't there: tears, sorrow, crying, pain, death. But what will be most significant is what *will* be there—Jesus.

The biblical understanding of sin helps us understand what hell will be like. The most common description of sin is self-centeredness. Since egocentrism is at the root of sin, we can surmise that it's also a part of hell. In fact, we could say sin causes us to shrink further and further into ourselves until we become nothing. This is not to advocate annihilationism (the destroying of all wicked people at death) but to help us understand that hell is utter, self-chosen aloneness. Total absence from God is the essence of hell. Hell is to be finally and utterly alone.

Scripture describes hell as a lake of fire burning with sulfur. This again portrays the unimaginable horror of eternal separation from God. However, hell is more than the absence of God. It is also experiencing God fully—but it is the experience of His divine wrath.

So, when will Christ return to judge the living and the dead? While many have attempted to give dates, or at least time periods, Wesleyans leave the future open. We do not believe God has all of eternity mapped out and has already decided when and how the Second Coming will occur. We believe human decisions do play some part in determining when and how Christ will return. In fact, 2 Peter 3:9-12 tells us two things concerning the return of Christ. First, God may delay Christ's return to allow more people to repent. Second, we can actually speed up Christ's return by living holy and godly lives.

Knowing this, the Christian's task is not to concern himself or herself with the time of Christ's return. The Christian's task is to be prepared for His return (Mark 13:33) and to invite others to be ready themselves.

Look It Up

1. Read 1 Corinthians 15:14. Why did Paul feel that if Christ had not been raised from the dead our faith was useless?

2. According to John 11:25-26, what happens when we believe in Jesus Christ?

3. Why does Jesus say in Matthew 24:36 that we need to keep watch?

 Big Words

Antichrist—A false leader who will come to power during the Tribulation claiming to be the Messiah. He will be defeated by Christ.

Millennium—A thousand-year time period when Christ will come to earth to reign.

Rapture—Refers to Jesus' return to earth in the end times when He will take His followers with Him to heaven. Those Christians who have died will rise first, then those Christians who are still alive will be taken up.

> **Did You Know?**
> When Jesus Christ came the first time, almost everyone missed Him because they were looking for a mighty king, but He came as a humble child. Maybe there is something we should learn from this regarding Christ's second coming.

Second Coming—Refers to the time when Jesus Christ will return to earth again.

Tribulation—A belief that the Church will go through a period of persecution lasting seven years. During this time, Israel will be persecuted, many people will turn to Christ, the Antichrist will become powerful and then will fall, and the world will end in a battle at a place called Armageddon.

 Why Should I Care?

Simply put, you should care because this topic affects your life for all of eternity. If we have asked Jesus Christ into our hearts, we can rest assured that during the final judgment, when our sins are laid out before us, everything that we have asked Jesus to forgive will have been forgotten. We will then be privileged to live with Him in heaven for all of eternity.

But, if we have not asked Jesus to forgive our sins, then we will be separated from those who have, and sent to hell. There we will live forever in total isolation from God and from others. We will also experience the fullness of God's anger.

It could be you have gotten this far in this book and still have not repented of your sins and asked Jesus Christ to save you. If that's the case, I can honestly think of no better time to become a Christian than right now. And when you do, you will have the assurance that when you stand before God at the Final Judgment He will invite you into His heaven.

My Place in the Story

When we are invited into the Story of God, we discover that we are part of a long history of people who've been obedient to God. While most of those people have died, we who are still alive will one day have the opportunity to meet them, to rejoice together with them, reflecting back on God's leading throughout history. Those who are a part of the Story of God do not fear death, for we recognize God's Story continues after our physical deaths on earth. When we arrive in heaven, we'll continue as active participants in this grand and glorious Story.

 Take It with You

So you also must be ready, because the Son of Man will come at an hour when you do not expect him (Matthew 24:44).

Giving It to God

Pray this prayer: *Father, I admit I don't know a lot about what will happen in the end. But I thank You that I can have the assurance that, come what may, I will spend eternity with You. Help me live each day in expectation of Your second coming. Amen.*

Dig Deeper

Here is a book that will be helpful if you want to do more studying on this important topic:

- *The Second Coming: A Wesleyan Approach to the Doctrine of Last Things* by H. Ray Dunning (Kansas City: Beacon Hill Press of Kansas City, 1995). (083-411-5255)

  A book by prominent Wesleyan scholars that is both readable and informative.

The Church
Not Just a Holy Huddle

🔴 Real Life

It was Friday, and the Pleasant Valley youth group had just returned from its spring break ski trip. The conditions had been perfect for skiing, with fresh snow having fallen just before the group arrived. Furthermore, the evening services had been incredible. The worship times were inspiring, and the speaker challenging. All in all, it was a great time.

For Chandra, the week was even more special. She'd been trying to share her faith with her best friend,

Mindy, for the last six months, ever since Chandra herself had accepted the Lord. Since Mindy was an avid skier, Chandra thought this trip would be the perfect opportunity to expose Mindy to the youth group and for Chandra to tell her about Jesus.

During one of the services, Mindy responded to the invitation, giving her heart to Jesus. Chandra was so excited!

But on Saturday, Chandra's excitement quickly tempered. She and Mindy were eating lunch together at the mall, and Chandra asked Mindy if she needed a ride to church on Sunday. Mindy's reply puzzled Chandra. "I don't think I'll be going," Mindy said. "I think I can be a Christian without going to church. After all, isn't being a Christian about me and my relationship with God? I think I can take care of that by myself."

💀 To Quote

The church is a gathering of people who have experienced Christ as the risen Lord.
—Maxie Dunnam, 20th-century author and college president

The Church is called holy, because it is holy, because every member thereof is holy . . . as He that called them is holy.
—John Wesley, 18th-century English evangelist and the father of Wesleyan theology

Chandra didn't push the topic any further, partly because she was so shocked, and partly because she herself had felt that way at times. Why *did* she go to church? What was its purpose? Chandra knew she needed to talk with someone and get some answers—fast!

Have you ever felt like Mindy? How about Chandra? Most of us go to church without really knowing why we go. This chapter is to help you understand not only why church should be so important in our lives but, more importantly, what our role in the church should be. Let's start with a few questions regarding our own beliefs about the Church.

 Your Life

1. What do you think is the purpose of the Church?

2. Do you think it's necessary for a Christian to go to church? Why, or why not?

3. On a scale from 1 to 10, how well do you think your local church acts like the Church Jesus established?

 Theology 101

What comes to your mind when you think of the word "church"? A building? A group of people who gather together to hear someone preach at them? Something that's boring and/or irrelevant to your life?

Unfortunately, too many people only have a negative image of the church. But that's usually because they don't really understand the purpose of the Church and what its role is.

There's a poem you might have recited when you were in kindergarten that had certain hand motions. Do you remember it?

"Here is the church, here is the steeple. Open the doors, and see all the people." Well, as fun as that poem might have been, it wasn't quite accurate. The Church is not just a building but is made up of individuals who've committed their lives to Jesus Christ. In other words, the Church is *not* the structure we meet in, but it's the people who come together to worship Christ. And the Church is much bigger than your local congregation, or even your denomination. The Church is not just the "here and now," but instead is comprised of all those who have lived before us, those who live with us, and all who will come after us. That is why the author of Hebrews could say that "we are surrounded by such a great cloud of witnesses" (Hebrews 12:1). He knew that those who have gone on before are as much a part of the Church as we are right now.

The Church's mission is to bring about the kingdom of God, and in so doing, to bring about the redemption of our world. What is this kingdom of God? It's not a place on a map; instead it's the attitude that seeks to follow God and be obedient to Him in all situations. However, we don't seek to bring the Kingdom in through coercion or the political process or even boycotts (although all of these have been tried in the past). Instead we seek to bring it into being by living lives of righteousness, sharing the Good News, practicing justice, and meeting the needs of those around us.

The Church exists in the world, but is not of this world. In fact, Scripture calls us "aliens and strangers" (1 Peter 2:11). However, this doesn't mean we completely separate ourselves from others. The Church is not designed to be a "holy huddle," seeking only to meet the needs of its members. Instead, it is the only organization that exists primarily for the purpose of its nonmembers. Its primary focus is to reach out in love to those who don't know Christ. This is what the Great Commission (Matthew 28:19-20) is all about. Yes, we must avoid those practices and lifestyles contrary to God's will, but we must also seek to build relationships with those who do not yet know Christ. We develop a genuine interest in others and their needs, and seek to meet those needs (physical, emotional, material, and spiritual) as the Body of Christ.

How do we meet those needs? The Lord gives the Church a variety of gifts that its members use to serve each other (for a list of those gifts see Romans 12, Ephesians 4, and 1 Corinthians 12). In particular, members have the opportunity, privilege, and responsibility to use their respective gifts for the benefit of others present. The Church needs to understand itself primarily as a community of believers whose calling is to be to others what Christ has been to them. A tall order, to be sure, but one we can accomplish because we are rooted in the vine (John 15:1-9).

So, can a person be a Christian without the Church? There have been isolated cases in history where someone has become a solitary monk and avoided contact with all others. I have no doubt that those people are in heaven today. But for most of us, we need the Church even more than it needs us. When we come to our local church, we come with the expectation that God will meet us there. We worship together, study the Bible, and engage in ministries to meet other's needs. We fellowship with one another and seek to provide encouragement and challenge. The Church becomes a place of safety and refuge, where we can come and know others will accept us regardless of our past. Furthermore, it's a place where all are welcome. Paul makes this point when he says we "are all one in Christ Jesus" (Galatians 3:28). The Church is often the one place where those of different racial, social, and economic backgrounds can come together under the unifying umbrella of knowing Jesus Christ as their Lord and Savior.

The Church isn't just another club we can choose to attend or not. Instead, it requires that we give all we have. In many ways, it's just like a family, seeking to help us grow and develop into what we were meant to be. The members of the Church serve as our mentors and teachers (in one sense, they are our parents, brothers, and sisters), helping us grow in our faith. This happens because the Church is composed of people who know the forces of sin and sin's consequences in their lives, but who also have experienced the forgiveness, the justification, the reconciliation, and the liberation of the risen Christ.

🔍 Look It Up

1. In Mark 1:15, John the Baptist announces to the people that the kingdom of God is at hand. What did he mean? Does the Church of today accurately reflect the kingdom of God?

2. According to 1 Peter 2:9-10, the Church is "a chosen people, a royal priesthood, a holy nation, a people belonging to God." List some specific ways that the Church can be each of these things.

3. According to 1 Corinthians 12:12-31, describe how the Church is like a body. What specific role(s) should you place in that body?

 ## Big Words

Body of Christ—A term used by the apostle Paul to describe the Church with emphasis on the unity and diversity of the Church. It also communicates that the Church is the continuing physical presence of Christ in the world.

Fellowship—Refers to the close relationship Christians share with one another and with God.

Kingdom of God—A phrase used by Jesus to summarize His teaching about the need for total obedience to God. It does not mean a geographical location, but a relationship of obedience.

DYK Did You Know?

The word "church" (little "c") refers to a local group of Christians who meet together weekly to worship God, study the Bible, and care for each other. "Church" (big "C") refers to all those who have ever lived who profess Jesus as their Savior.

 ## Why Should I Care?

All of us seek someplace where we can belong. We desire a place where we can come and feel safe and accepted. We want a place that understands us and wants the best for us. In addition, we need a place that can help us make our lives mean something.

The Church is the only place that can truly meet all of these needs. Through the care and concern of its members, and through the transforming work of God, we come to realize we are truly whole and complete when we are a part of God's kingdom.

We also desire to be a part of something much bigger than ourselves. Again the Church can help us here. When Christ established His Church on earth, He told Peter that "on this rock [Peter's confession of Christ] I will build my church" (Matthew 16:18). In other words, Christ needs us to do His work. He has chosen us and laid before us the challenge of reaching the world with the gospel. The question is, will we join Him in this magnificent quest, or will we be content to just wait around, hoping something better comes along? To paraphrase a popular slogan, the Church allows you to be all that you were created to be. Decide today to be a part of this great enterprise.

 ## My Place in the Story

As Christians, we believe we are a Story-formed community, a people on a common journey. When we join this community of God, we find we are connected to something much bigger than our own lives. We participate in the same Story that includes Abraham, Paul, Luther, Wesley, and Mother Teresa. What a tremendous thought— God chooses to invite us to be a part of furthering His kingdom through our participation in this Story!

 ## Giving It to God

Pray this prayer: *Father, I must confess I don't understand why You would choose to use me to further Your kingdom. But please know that I eagerly desire to be a part of this Kingdom. Give me the grace I require to accomplish Your will, and give me the necessary mercy to meet those needs You show me. Help me live my life in such a way that when others see me, they will see You. In Jesus' name. Amen.*

Take It with You

But you are a chosen people, a royal priesthood, a holy nation, a people belonging to God, that you may declare the praises of him who called you out of darkness into his wonderful light. Once you were not a people, but now you are the people of God; once you had not received mercy, but now you have received mercy (1 Peter 2:9-10).

Dig Deeper

Here are some books that will be helpful if you want to do more studying on this important topic:

- *Life Together* by Dietrich Bonhoeffer (San Francisco: Harper, 1954). (006-060-8528)

    Bonhoeffer was a pastor in Germany while Hitler was in power and was a prophetic voice of what the Church should be like. An incredible book.

- *The Community of the King* by Howard Snyder (Downers Grove, Ill.: InterVarsity Press, 1978). (087-784-7525)

    A book that looks at what the kingdom of God is about, and how the current Church measures up.

9

Sacraments
Acting Out What God's Doing on the Inside!

 Real Life

As Stewart and Juan went through the lunch line, they both decided to have the pizza. While it was sometimes undercooked, it looked much better than the other choice—"mystery meat."

After finding a table, they sat down and began talking about what had happened at church yesterday.

"Hey, wasn't yesterday just incredible?" Juan asked. "First, we have a baptism service in the morning, and then last night we had Communion. What a combination!"

Stewart hesitated just a moment. Should he reveal to Juan that he didn't understand why a bunch of people had gotten wet, nor did he know why they made such a big fuss about eating a cracker and drinking a thimbleful of juice? Juan was his best friend, so he decided to risk it.

"To tell you the truth, I was confused. I don't understand why we practice baptism and Communion. What's the purpose? What do they do for us? Do you have to be a Christian for a long time before you understand these things?"

To Quote

There is but one scriptural way wherein we receive inward grace—through the outward means which God hath appointed.
—John Wesley, 18th-century English evangelist and the father of Wesleyan theology

There is beauty, to be sure, in the sacraments, but the beauty lies in the majesty with which God goes his way in history, making earthly elements to become sacraments by his word.
—G. C. Berkouwer, 20th-century theologian

Juan suppressed a smile. He knew Stewart had only been a Christian for a short period of time. In fact, Juan had been the one to lead Stewart to Christ. And while Stewart had been very hungry and eager to grow, there were still a lot of things he had to learn.

"I'm sorry," Juan said. "I guess I sometimes forget you haven't been a Christian very long and don't know about these things. Both baptism and the Lord's Supper are holy sacraments that we in the Church practice. Let me see if I can explain them to you."

Have you ever felt like Stewart, not really understanding why the Church does some things? The Church does a few things that, to the outsider, don't seem to make much sense. For that matter, sometimes even to new Christians the actions may not make any sense unless the person has been told why the actions are important.

In this chapter, we will be looking at two things that, while the world doesn't understand them, are very important to the life of the Church: the acts of baptism and the Lord's Supper.

 ## Your Life

1. In 50 words or less, tell what you know about baptism.

2. In 50 words or less, tell what you know about the Lord's Supper.

 ## Theology 101

Have you ever heard the word "sacrament" used in church, but you didn't know what it meant? In Protestant doctrine, a sacrament is an action that involves an outward sign accompanied by a promise of forgiveness for sins. When received in faith, it becomes a means of grace. Still confused? Try this: a sacrament is an outward sign of an inward action. In other words, we do something on the outside to represent what God is doing or has done on the inside.

Sacraments are not just dry and lifeless rituals you do for big occasions and holidays. Instead, sacraments are very meaningful not only because of the action they symbolize but also because in a sacrament we make a promise to God and He makes a promise to us. In the act of the sacrament, God is able to give us His grace to sustain us spiritually.

Throughout history, God has used physical things to represent spiritual things happening in our lives. In the Old Testament, there were two of these important acts. One was circumcision, which symbolized that one was a Jew and a member of God's family. The other was the Passover meal, which was eaten as a remembrance of God's deliverance of Israel from their Egyptian captors.

When Jesus came, He instituted two new symbolic actions that Christians were to participate in. Baptism replaced circumcision as an indication of being incorporated into God's family, and the Lord's Supper replaced the Passover meal as a remembrance of God's deliverance of us, not just from earthly forces, but from sin as well.

While the Catholic Church and some others acknowledge seven sacraments, baptism and the Lord's Supper are the only two sacraments Protestants practice. This is because they are the only two that the Lord commanded and that also carry a promise of forgiveness. Let's examine each of these to get a better picture of why they are important.

Baptism (Not just another dip in the pool!)

Jesus set the example we all should follow when He was baptized himself (see Matthew 3:13-17). Later, when Jesus sent His disciples out, He instructed them to baptize all who became disciples.

We are to be baptized after we have taken the first step in our relationship with Jesus Christ and have been born again. Baptism does not save a sinner but shows that the sinner has already been forgiven of his or her sins and is now a disciple of Jesus. Baptism symbolizes the change and new life that God has given us.

However, baptism is more than just a symbolic ritual; it also has deep significance for our spiritual life. Some scholars call baptism the sacrament of "initiation." In baptism, a person is symbolically initiated into the family of God! While technically that person is already a part of God's family the moment he or she is saved, baptism is a time for that person and others to visually see and celebrate this fact.

When Christians go down into the water, they become identified with Christ's death, and when they come up from the water, they identify with Christ's resurrected life. In baptism we are acting out what we already know and believe in our hearts—that Jesus Christ died for our sins and was resurrected three days later.

There are different ways in which you can be baptized. Many Christians choose to be lowered completely under the water (what is called "immersion"). Others have water poured or sprinkled over their heads. The only specific Scripture offers is that we are to be baptized in the name of the Father, Son, and Holy Spirit.

Technically, a person doesn't have to be baptized to be saved. This means you don't have to be scared if you haven't been baptized yet! But if you are excited about your relationship with Christ and what He has done for you, baptism should be something you want to do and look forward to doing.

The Lord's Supper (More than just juice and crackers!)

If baptism is the sacrament that initiates one into the Church and signifies the identifying of oneself with Christ, the Lord's Supper is the sacrament that celebrates the continuance of this relationship as well as serving to perpetuate it.

The Lord's Supper was instituted by Christ himself during the last meal He shared with His disciples (just before His arrest and trial). At that meal, He broke bread and gave it to His disciples to eat. He then poured wine, passed it, and gave it to them to drink. Christ asked His disciples to do these things as a remembrance of Him.

When we partake of the Lord's Supper, we are called to remember and celebrate what Christ has done for us. In fact, another of the words we often substitute for the Lord's Supper is the Eucharist. The word "Eucharist" means "giving thanks." Every time we partake, we should remember what Christ has done for us and be thankful.

The Lord's Supper is a visible symbol of the presence of Christ. The bread represents the body of Christ, which was broken for us. The juice represents His blood, which was spilled for our salvation. Every time we partake, we symbolically observe His body and blood given for us. In those moments when we feel like Christ is far away, we can come to the table and, holding those elements, know Christ is just as present with us as He was with His disciples. Another word commonly used to describe the Lord's Supper is "Communion," which means "fellowship" or "participation."

The Lord's Supper is also a proclamation. We proclaim what

Christ has done for us and what He will do. Every time we eat and drink of the cup, we are spreading the gospel message.

The sacrament of the Lord's Supper is a symbol of fellowship. Acknowledgment of our common need breaks down all racial, social, and cultural barriers. A professor of mine used to say that at the foot of the Cross, we all stand on equal ground.

When we participate in the Lord's Supper, we receive renewal, commitment, and spiritual comfort. We need this because being saved is not the end. Instead, we continue to grow in Christ. In fact, Wesley viewed the Lord's Supper as a means of grace essential to keeping the conversion process alive. When we participate, we receive all we need to grow in Christ.

 ## Look It Up

1. Look up Matthew 28:19-20. Why does Jesus command the disciples to baptize in "the name of the Father and of the Son and of the Holy Spirit"?

2. In 1 Corinthians 11:28, the apostle Paul says that a person should always examine himself or herself before participating in the Lord's Supper. Why is this so important?

 ## Big Words

Baptism—A symbolic action using water that a believer participates in as a visible sign that the person is a Christian.

Faith—A response of trust in God in which a Christian not only believes in God but acts on that belief in obedience.

 Did You Know?

In the earliest days of the Church, baptism was a much longer process. Candidates for baptism had to have come through a three-year period of worship and instruction before being baptized. After that period, their lives were examined to see if they truly lived out the essence of the gospel. If so, they were then eligible for baptism.

When they were baptized, they were required to take off everything—including their clothes! This was to symbolize that they were taking nothing of their old way of life with them into this new life signified by baptism. I guess it's a good thing some things change over the years!

Lord's Supper—The act of remembering the death and sharing in the life and sufferings of Christ by eating the bread, which represents Christ's body and drinking the juice, which represents His blood. Also commonly referred to as the "Eucharist" or "Communion."

 ## Why Should I Care?

As stated above, both baptism and the Lord's Supper are means of grace. In other words, they are avenues through which God conveys to us spiritual life and strength for daily living.

Every Christian we know needs as much of God's strength and grace as he or she can possibly get. It's a rough world out there, with many people and things trying to pull you away from God. The only way we can succeed spiritually is to regularly replenish our souls with what God offers us. In the sacraments of baptism and the Lord's Supper, we have two of the best sources from which to feed.

If you have not yet been baptized, talk to your pastor or youth pastor about participating in this important event. And if you have not participated in the Lord's Supper up till now, then the next time your church offers it, partake of the bread and juice. Most importantly, be open to what God wants to teach you through these two means of grace.

 ## My Place in the Story

Baptism and the Lord's Supper have served as means of grace throughout the history of the Church. These historical practices remind us that we are a part of the ongoing Story of God. Every time we partake of the Lord's Supper, we in effect retell the story of God's love for us. We rejoice in that grace so freely offered. Every time someone in the community of faith chooses to be baptized, he or she is initiated and adopted into God's family, which includes all who have come before us. These practices remind us of God's presence in our midst

 Take It with You

He saved us, not because of righteous things we had done, but because of his mercy. He saved us through the washing of rebirth and renewal by the Holy Spirit (Titus 3:5).

Whenever you eat this bread and drink this cup, you proclaim the Lord's death until he comes (1 Corinthians 11:26).

and give us the grace necessary to remain active participants in the Story.

 Giving It to God

Pray this prayer: *Gracious God, I want to know You more. I understand participating in baptism and in Your special meal are two ways in which I can know You better. As I participate, teach me Your truth, and impart to me Your grace. Amen.*

Here are some books that will be helpful if you want to do more studying on this important topic:

- *Remember Who You Are: Baptism, a Model for Christian Life* by William Willimon (Nashville: Upper Room, 1980). (068-760-9739)

  A delightful book that explains the significance of our baptism.

- *Sunday Dinner: The Lord's Supper and the Christian Life* by William Willimon (Nashville: Upper Room, 1991). (068-761-1148)

  This book gives a clear and enjoyable explanation of the significance of the Lord's Supper.

ALMOST THE END

Congratulations! You finished the book. The hours you've invested in this study were well-used, and you have learned a lot. It could be that, for the first time in your life, you finally understand what it means to be a Christian. The question is, what are you going to do about it?

You see, reading and understanding this book is important. It's necessary for you to know not only *what* you believe but *why* you believe as well. That way you'll be confident in your own faith and beliefs. Furthermore, as 1 Peter 3:15 states, you will "always be prepared to give an answer to everyone who asks you to give the reason for the hope that you have."

But equally important is how you live out these truths. It doesn't matter how much you know if you only keep it as head knowledge and don't allow it to become heart knowledge. There have been countless numbers of people who've only studied the Scriptures and the Christian faith to secure knowledge, but have never allowed it to change their lives. One powerful example of this was given by Scott Udell in *Psychology Today*.[1] Udell tells the story of the prince of Grenada, an heir to the Spanish crown, who was sentenced to spend the rest of his life in solitary confinement in a prison. During his time in prison, he was given only one book to read—the Bible. To help spend his time, he read and reread the Bible literally hundreds of times during his 33 years of imprisonment.

When he died, and the jailers came in to take his body out, they discovered something unusual. Using a couple of nails he'd found in the cell, the prince had scratched notes on the prison wall regarding what he had learned from his years of Bible study. However, all the notes were of this type: Psalm 118:8 is the middle verse of the Bible; Ezra 7:21 contains all the letters of the alphabet except the letter *j*; Esther 8:9 is the longest verse in the Bible.

Even though he'd spent 33 years studying the "living and active" Word of God (Hebrews 4:12), he had learned nothing more than trivia. He hadn't allowed the Bible to impact his life.

You see, friends won't ask you to "give the reason" for this hope you have if you aren't living it out before them. Furthermore, you must show genuine care for them, building a relationship with them based on God's love. There's an old saying that may be trite, but it certainly is true—Your friends won't care how much you know until they know how much you care.

Don't be alarmed if your friends (or others) ask questions that you can't answer. As we learned in the chapter on the Trinity, there are some things about God that are a mystery. You're going to have some questions that remain unanswered, and that's OK. In fact, lots of people who study the Bible and theology full-time have unanswered questions. They just aren't willing to admit it!

We have to remember that the Christian life is a long journey. There are things we just won't learn until we've been Christians for a while. There are other things, such as the topics in this book, that we can begin to understand right now.

The key to continued growth as Christians is continual examination of our faith, to keep asking questions, in an effort to learn all that we can about God and His relationship with us. It's when we stop asking the questions and seeking answers about God that we need to worry about losing our faith.

Throughout this book we've covered nine beliefs that are central to the Christian faith. It took us almost 100 pages to effectively cover it. However, almost two centuries ago, an effort was made to summarize the central beliefs of Christianity into a creed. What we know today as the Apostles' Creed is the result of that effort.

We encourage you to memorize this creed. Yes, we know it's a little long. But just as the Scripture verses you memorized in this book can guide your way, this creed can continually remind you what Christians throughout the centuries have held to as their core beliefs. May it guide and inspire you just as it has Christians for nearly 2,000 years. We offer it here as our concluding thoughts on this subject of vital beliefs.

THE APOSTLES' CREED

I believe in God the Father Almighty,
    Maker of heaven and earth;
And in Jesus Christ, His only Son, our Lord;
    who was conceived by the Holy Spirit,
        born of the Virgin Mary,
        suffered under Pontius Pilate,
        was crucified, dead, and buried;
        He descended into hades;
    the third day He rose again from the dead;
    He ascended into heaven,
        and sitteth at the right hand of God the Father Almighty;
    from thence He shall come to judge the living and the dead.
I believe in the Holy Spirit,
    the holy Church universal,
    the communion of saints,
    the forgiveness of sins,
    the resurrection of the body,
    and the life everlasting. Amen.

NOTES

Finding Our Place in the Story

1. *The Works of John Wesley*, 3rd ed. (Kansas City: Beacon Hill Press of Kansas City), 1:74.

2. Ibid., 103.

Chapter 1

1. J. Kenneth Grider, "The Holy Trinity: The Triune God" in *A Contemporary Wesleyan Theology*, ed. Charles W. Carter (Grand Rapids: Francis Asbury Press, 1983), 378.

Chapter 4

1. Brennan Manning, *The Ragamuffin Gospel* (Portland, Oreg.: Multnomah Press, 1990), 116-17.

Chapter 6

1. C. S. Lewis, *The Problem of Pain* (Nashville: Broadman and Holman, 1999).

Almost the End

1. Wayne Rice, *Hot Illustrations for Youth Talks* (El Cajon, Calif.: Youth Specialties Books, 1994).